Contents

C000089011

WOULD YOU RATHER LEGENDARY: The Complete collection of hilarious hypothetical questions

- By Clint Hammerstrike

About the Author

Someone with plenty of free time to write this book and enough imagination to make up the name Clint Hammerstrike – seriously why wouldn't you!

What else is there to say other than you will be pleased to know this isn't my day job!

Introduction

Writing all these book has been one of the most enjoyable things that I have ever done (I live a very dull life – cue the worlds tiniest violin)! This is because I have spent a lifetime pondering random scenarios and questions. If I had a pound for every time I had contemplated the questions would I rather X OR Y, I would be richer than Scrooge McDuck (but I would rather be poor and be Mickey Mouse).

I wrote this book to share with you all the wisdom I have amassed writing all these books including some of the great conundrums we face as humanity such as: Would you rather brush your teeth with a rat OR a Pigeon? Would you rather have all your meals covered in gravy OR cheese for a year? Would you rather carry hot soup in your hands OR a lobster in your underwear? This book will also help you sort your wreck of a life out by exploring important life scenarios such as:

Remember all of these scenarios are for hypothetical entertainment purposes and should not be taken as a recommendation or an endorsement. You should never lick a toilet (no matter it's state of cleanliness), kick your partners mother in shins, or use an old-age pensioner as a weapon to fight off Zombie Koalas. Did I really need to say that last sentence!?!

Helpful Guide

To aid you on this journey of self-discovery I have suggested a couple of rules to help you through.

Rule 1: You must answer. Even if you would rather do neither you MUST pick!

Rule 2: Don't rush your answer. Give yourself time to consider the sheer complexity and horror of the choice!

Rule 3: Respect the opinion of those reading with you? Even when they are plainly wrong!

Rule 4: Take this seriously, we are considering the meaning of life do not even consider laughing!

Rule 5: Forget rule 4. Laugh, come on its sucking on a marathon runners sock OR licking a goats face. Enough said!

WOULD YOU RATHER RANDOMS: A collection of hilarious hypothetical questions

- By Clint Hammerstrike

Chapter one: Nice and Simple

WOULD YOU RATHER:

Have a hairy nose OR hairy ears?

WOULD YOU RATHER:

Always have a runny nose OR a cough?

WOULD YOU RATHER:

Make the sound of a cat OR a dog when you fart?

WOULD YOU RATHER:

Bite your tongue OR stub your toe?

WOULD YOU RATHER:

Constantly smell really bad but not be able to smell yourself (everyone else can) OR be constantly surrounded by an awful stench that you can smell (but you don't smell)?

WOULD YOU RATHER:

Brush your teeth with a rat OR a pigeon?

WOULD YOU RATHER:

Cry cola OR chocolate milk tears?

WOULD YOU RATHER:

Always be hungry OR thirsty?

WOULD YOU RATHER:

Suck on a marathon runners sock OR lick a goat's face?

WOULD YOU RATHER:

Eat the contents of a spot OR a blister?

WOULD YOU RATHER:

Only be able to eat food that was too spicy OR too salty?

WOULD YOU RATHER:

Be able to make people cry OR laugh by touching them?

WOULD YOU RATHER:

Be a vampire OR a werewolf?

WOULD YOU RATHER:

Be able to read people's minds OR control people's minds?

WOULD YOU RATHER:

Have £1million pounds that you could only spend on other people OR £20,000 that you could only spend on yourself?

WOULD YOU RATHER:

Have a Ferrari and not be able to drive it OR a Vauxhall Corsa and be able to drive it?

WOULD YOU RATHER:

Sleep without a pillow OR a duvet?

WOULD YOU RATHER:

Catch a hedgehog OR a skunk falling from a tower block?

WOULD YOU RATHER:

Be trapped in a lift with a couple kissing OR fighting?

WOULD YOU RATHER:

Climb to the top of Everest OR win an Olympic Gold Medal?

WOULD YOU RATHER:

Never have to shower again OR never have to change your clothes again?

WOULD YOU RATHER:

Live in the White House OR Buckingham Palace?

WOULD YOU RATHER:

Be able to breakdance OR rap?

You are really hungry after another kale smoothie cleanse. Luckily for you a new restaurant has opened up in town. You are invited out by friends to try the new tasting menu where you get to pick each course. Calories don't count so let yourself go. What would you choose for:

- First Starter?

- Second Starter?

- First Main?

- Second Main?

- Third Main?

- First Dessert?

- Second Dessert?

- Third Dessert?

- Drink Number 1?

- Drink Number 2?

You go out for a walk one day and fall off a cliff. Thankfully science can rebuild you, but not as you once were. Using ground breaking technology scientist can mix animal body parts together to give you a new body. Luckily you can pick which animal for each part. What do you choose:

- Toes?

- Feet?

- Legs?

- Torso?

- Fingers?

- Arms?

- Neck?

- Face?

- Hair?

- Voice?

Life is hard and you deserve a holiday. But who can be bothered to go to the effort of booking a holiday. Isn't it much easier to just hand your credit card and pin number over to a strange man with a globe and a trench coat and let him plan it for you. Kindly he has provided a couple of options for you to choose from. If you're going to make your friends jealous on Facebook and Instagram, you better choose wisely. So would you rather go on holiday to:

- A Russian military prison OR a donkey waxing camp?
- A silent retreat OR a theme park?
- A relaxing beach holiday OR a skiing trip?
- A tropical jungle adventure OR a snowy mountain expedition?
- Inner city Birmingham OR Slough?
- Inter-railing through Europe OR backpacking across Australia?
- A steam train convention in Basingstoke OR an intensive cross-stitch course in Stoke?
- Clubbing in Ibiza OR sightseeing in Venice?
- New York OR Johannesburg?
- A monkey OR polar bear sanctuary?

It is Sunday evening and you are hungry. As you scavenge through the cupboards and fridge you curse the fact that your online groceries aren't being delivered until tomorrow. Looks like you are going to have to come up with some creative combinations. So would you rather eat:

- Tuna and marmite OR cheese and gravy?

- Jam and kale OR cornflakes and mayonnaise?

- A lemon and instant noodles OR tomato sauce and banana?

- Bread and jelly OR pasta and chocolate sauce?

- Spinach and honey OR satsuma and pickle?

- Cucumber and Pop Tarts OR tomato soup and porridge?

- Egg and peanut butter OR tofu and bacon?

- Curry paste and strawberries OR ice cream and rice?

- Cream cheese and chocolate spread OR mushrooms and popcorn?

- Potato and Haribo OR couscous and marshmallow fluff?

Chapter Two: Slightly harder

WOULD YOU RATHER:

Always be too hot OR too cold?

WOULD YOU RATHER:

Have the neck of a giraffe OR the flippers of a penguin?

WOULD YOU RATHER:

Never have to poo OR be sick again?

WOULD YOU RATHER:

Have eyes on your elbows OR a mouth on your stomach?

WOULD YOU RATHER:

Have no eyes but still be able to see OR no nose and still be able to smell?

WOULD YOU RATHER:

Have an itch that you can't scratch OR a sneeze that won't come out?

WOULD YOU RATHER:

Sneeze out of your bottom OR fart out of your mouth?

WOULD YOU RATHER:

Have a toe for a tongue OR tongues for toes?

WOULD YOU RATHER:

Have all your meals for a year covered in cheese OR gravy?

WOULD YOU RATHER:

Eat a hotdog with chocolate sauce on it OR an ice cream with ketchup on it?

WOULD YOU RATHER:

Eat 10 caterpillars OR have to wear them as a necklace for a day?

WOULD YOU RATHER:

Only eat stuffing for the rest of your life OR only drink gravy for the rest of your life?

WOULD YOU RATHER:

Eat a puppy that tastes like chocolate OR a kitten that tastes like strawberries?

WOULD YOU RATHER:

Be the fastest person in the wold OR the strongest?

WOULD YOU RATHER:

Be able to stop time OR travel back in time?

WOULD YOU RATHER:

Only be able to communicate by singing OR whispering in people's ears?

WOULD YOU RATHER:

Have to carry hot soup in your hands OR a lobster in your underwear?

WOULD YOU RATHER:

Wear wet socks for a day OR an itchy woollen jumper?

WOULD YOU RATHER:

Wear someone else's used underwear OR use someone else's toothbrush?

WOULD YOU RATHER:

Always have to answer truthfully OR always lie?

WOULD YOU RATHER:

Fight off a dog sized rat OR a cow sized ant?

WOULD YOU RATHER:

Lie in a bath of spiders OR snakes?

WOULD YOU RATHER:

Remember everything (and not be able to forget) OR be able to completely forget anything?

WOULD YOU RATHER:

Have to speak everything on your mind OR never be able to speak again?

WOULD YOU RATHER:

Know how you're going to die OR when you're going to die?

WOULD YOU RATHER:

Be the cleverest person in a room OR the funniest?

Rocky, The Sound of Music and Top Gun what do they all have in common other than being adrenaline junkie movies? That's right a killer soundtrack. So why should you have to walk around like an extra rather than a movie star. It's time to give your life a re-make! What song would you rather hear rising from the background at these key moments:

- Being born?

- Growing up?

- First Kiss?

- Graduation?

- First Job?

- Wedding?

- First Child?

- Middle Age?

- Growing Old?

- Death Scene?

You have been training for this for weeks, doing sit-ups, playing old school Tekken and eating Beef Jerky. You find yourself in the ring and the crowd are cheering. You are ready to fight, now you just have to select your opponent. So would you rather fight:

- Peppa Pig OR Tinky Winky?

- A lion sized koala OR a koala sized lion?

- Seventy, five year olds OR five, seventy year olds?

- Your mum OR your partner?

- A granny OR a puppy?

- A politician OR a banker?

- A dentist OR a traffic warden?

- A Dachshund sized T-Rex OR a T-Rex sized Dachshund?

- Thor OR The Hulk?

- A heavyweight boxer OR a Sumo Wrestler?

Money is tight and you have to find a way to pay the bills. Medical experimentation is the way to go – Am I right??? You sign up at the clinic and change into a gown that doesn't hide your backside (what's the deal with that?). A doctor hands you a clipboard for you to select the trials you would like to take part in. Picking the wrong one could have some uncomfortable side effects. So would you rather side effects that:

- Make you talk in in Taylor Swift Lyrics OR Yoda quotes?
- Make you see in black and white OR hear everyone speaking like Ned Flanders?
- Make your urine rainbow coloured OR smell like strawberries?
- Make you punch yourself every time you blink OR kick yourself every time fifth breath you take?
- Make you sound like Darth Vader OR Elmo?
- Make you irresistible to Camels OR Llamas?
- Make you able to break dance OR speak another language?
- Change your hands to pizza wheels OR sparklers?
- Give you cravings for sand OR dry skin flakes?
- Make you cry when you should laugh OR laugh when you should cry?

Regrets? Self-loathing? Asking yourself what am I doing with my life (issues I have asked myself writing this book)! Wouldn't it be easier if I could just start all over again? Wouldn't it be better if you were a part time Barista/full time sky diver? Who says a leopard can't change its spots? It's time to sort out your life. So would you rather:

- Stop world hunger OR find a cure for cancer?

- Bring an end to all wars OR end global poverty?

- Adopt a litter of kittens OR a litter of puppies?

- Be a spy OR a doctor?

- Be a poet OR a mime artist?

- Own a bakery OR a sweet shop?

- Be the president of the USA OR Queen/King of England?

- Have a number one hit song OR number one box office movie?

- Be a painter OR an author?

- Save the earth from a meteor OR an alien invasion?

Chapter Three: Hmm that's tricky

WOULD YOU RATHER:

Have Pool balls for eyes OR Dominoes for teeth?

WOULD YOU RATHER:

Sweat melted cheese OR chocolate sauce?

WOULD YOU RATHER:

Have a head twice as small OR twice as big?

WOULD YOU RATHER:

Have the ears of a bunny OR the tail of a horse?

WOULD YOU RATHER:

Have the fur of a bear OR the feathers of a flamingo?

WOULD YOU RATHER:

Eat through your bottom OR poo through your mouth?

WOULD YOU RATHER:

Use eye drops made of chilli sauce OR toilet paper made of sandpaper?

WOULD YOU RATHER:

Eat your toe OR your finger?

WOULD YOU RATHER:

Drink lemonade through your nose OR your eyes?

WOULD YOU RATHER:

Be fed spoon-fed dinner by Dracula OR Voldemort?

WOULD YOU RATHER:

Have all sweet food taste savoury OR all savoury food taste sweet?

WOULD YOU RATHER:

Eat food that has been pre-chewed by a stranger OR a dog?

WOULD YOU RATHER:

Be able to drink lava OR eat metal?

WOULD YOU RATHER:

Be able to run super-fast OR slow time down?

WOULD YOU RATHER:

Be able to swim like a shark OR run like a cheetah?

WOULD YOU RATHER:

No one turns up for your wedding OR your funeral?

WOULD YOU RATHER:

Be able to speak every language OR communicate with animals?

WOULD YOU RATHER:

Always get away with lying OR always know when someone is lying to you?

WOULD YOU RATHER:

Speak every language OR play every musical instrument?

WOULD YOU RATHER:

Be trapped in space OR at the bottom of the ocean?

WOULD YOU RATHER:

Always have a terrible song stuck in your head OR have the same nightmare each night?

WOULD YOU RATHER:

Raise sheep for eggs OR chickens for wool?

WOULD YOU RATHER:

Be the best player on a losing team OR the worst player on a winning team?

WOULD YOU RATHER:

Stand up and sing in-front of a group of work colleagues OR strangers?

WOULD YOU RATHER:

Not be able to access the internet OR not see anyone for a month?

Your new kitchen has been installed and you are ready to get your apron on and create a gastronomic marvel. But you can't keep this decadent feast to yourself you need some dinner guests. The question is who should you invite? You flick through your endless contacts list but who would you rather invite from these categories:

- A sport person?

- A film star?

- A musician?

- A dead person from history (not decomposed and fit for the dinner table)?

- A family Member?

- A friend?

- A cartoon character?

- A superhero?

- A fictional character?

- One freebie choice?

On a lovely day trip out you fall into a nuclear reactor. Somehow you survive the brutal gamma raysAs you clench tight trying to avoid becoming a green rage filled beast you face the choice of what superpowers you will take on. Remember with great power comes great responsibility! So, would you rather:

- Be a superhero OR a supervillain?

- Be invisible OR able to fly?

- Age at half the speed OR run 100 times the speed of a normal human?

- Be able to lift up lorries with your hands OR with your mind?

- Be able to create fire OR ice?

- Be able to stretch to incredible lengths OR shrink to microscopic size?

- Have x-ray vision OR supersonic hearing?

- Be able to shoot lasers out of your eyes OR spider webs from your hands?

- Be able to move things with your mind OR control people's minds?

- Be super strong OR super smart?

You are walking down the street. As you enter the door of your local convenience store you are sucked into a Freaky Friday/13 again Vortex where you inhabit the body of a random person. Fortunately for you, you have some choice as to whose body that is. Pick well or suffer. So, would you rather be:

- Donald Trump OR a knife throwers assistant?

- A naked jellyfish handler OR a scorpion juggler?

- Your mum OR your dad?

- You 10 years ago OR you 10 years in the future?

- King Kong OR Godzilla?

- A dentist that has to give the Hulk root canal OR the hygiene therapist that has to give the Hulk a colonic?

- The tallest person in the world OR the shortest?

- A cast member from "The Only Way is Essex" OR "Made in Chelsea"?

- A medical trial participant for a laxatives company OR the cleaner for a laxative trial company?

- A member of the Mafia OR the Yakuza?

Chapter Four: Oh gosh help me

WOULD YOU RATHER:

Have six fingers on each hand OR 8 toes on each foot?

WOULD YOU RATHER:

Wear a snowsuit in the Sahara Desert OR be naked at the North Pole?

WOULD YOU RATHER:

Get a paper cut OR bite your tongue?

WOULD YOU RATHER:

Have fingers as long as your arms OR arms as long as your fingers?

WOULD YOU RATHER:

Have toes OR fingers like curly fries?

WOULD YOU RATHER:

Poo yourself every time someone says your name OR wet yourself every time you cough?

WOULD YOU RATHER:

When you squeeze a spot a whole tub of cream cheese comes out OR a slug?

WOULD YOU RATHER:

Spend the rest of your life with Wotsit dust on your hands OR sand in-between your toes?

WOULD YOU RATHER:

Eat your favourite meal for the rest of your life OR never again?

WOULD YOU RATHER:

Give up chocolate OR alcohol?

WOULD YOU RATHER:

Eat a loaf of mouldy bread OR drink a pint of gone off milk?

WOULD YOU RATHER:

Lick a stranger's armpit OR eat their snot?

WOULD YOU RATHER:

Be able to fly like a bird OR swim like a shark?

WOULD YOU RATHER:

Everything you think becomes true OR be able to control people with a PlayStation controller?

WOULD YOU RATHER:

Be Superman OR Batman?

WOULD YOU RATHER:

Live where it is constantly winter OR summer?

WOULD YOU RATHER:

Spend the rest of your life on a plane OR a boat?

WOULD YOU RATHER:

Spend twenty years in prison and then be found innocent OR be put away for 15 years (be innocent) but be considered guilty forever?

WOULD YOU RATHER:

Never eat chocolate OR never use a smartphone?

WOULD YOU RATHER:

Be stung by a jellyfish OR give up social media for 6 months?

WOULD YOU RATHER:

Be allergic to carbohydrates OR the internet?

WOULD YOU RATHER:

Lose all your photos OR all your technology?

WOULD YOU RATHER:

Go back into the past to meet your ancestors OR forward into the future to meet your great-great-great-great grandchildren?

WOULD YOU RATHER:

Get rich working hard OR winning the lottery?

WOULD YOU RATHER:

Hear the good news first OR the bad news first?

Life is stressful and you deserve a relaxing bath. You put in your bath bomb, light a candle and turn on some whale music. You leave the bath running whilst you finish your stamp collection. But those stamps are so entertaining that you lose track of time. Next thing you know a tidal wave is coming out of the bathroom. In a few minutes your house will be ruined but you have time to save some possessions. The question is would you rather save:

- Your clothes OR your TV?

- Your smartphone OR your pet?

- Your photos OR your love letters?

- Your bed OR your sofa?

- Your laptop OR your tablet?

- Your fridge OR your oven?

- Your books OR your DVDs?

- Your watch OR your camera?

- Your wallet or your car keys?

- Your games console OR wedding album?

Chapter Five: I Surrender

WOULD YOU RATHER:

Always be sticky OR itchy?

WOULD YOU RATHER:

Have explosive diarrhoea OR projectile vomit?

WOULD YOU RATHER:

Bathe in other people's sweat -but come out clean OR never shower again and be smelly?

WOULD YOU RATHER:

Poo yourself every day for a month but nobody know OR poo yourself once and everybody know?

WOULD YOU RATHER:

Not be able to clean your teeth OR your armpits for a year?

WOULD YOU RATHER:

Have a 10 inch "innie" bellybutton OR a 10 inch "outie" bellybutton?

WOULD YOU RATHER:

Eat your food with your feet OR blow your nose with your tongue?

WOULD YOU RATHER:

Drink bin juice OR eat a stranger's fingernail clippings?

WOULD YOU RATHER:

All your food has toenails in it OR hair?

WOULD YOU RATHER:

Be Spider-man OR Ant-man?

WOULD YOU RATHER:

Be stupid in a world of clever people OR be clever in a world of stupid people?

WOULD YOU RATHER:

Only be able to speak in song OR only say 100 words in a day?

WOULD YOU RATHER:

Be able to spit custard OR mayonnaise?

WOULD YOU RATHER:

Win £50,000 OR your friend wins £500,000?

WOULD YOU RATHER:

Have a dog with a human face OR a cat with human hands?

WOULD YOU RATHER:

Have to touch someone with your nose every time you talk to them OR give them a foot rub when the conversation ends?

WOULD YOU RATHER:

Be stuck behind a slow walker OR have a stone in your shoe?

WOULD YOU RATHER:

Have to wear a Bikini/Mankini all the time OR never change your underwear again?

WOULD YOU RATHER:

Never be allowed inside OR outside?

WOULD YOU RATHER:

Wear clown clothes OR clown make up for the rest of your life?

WOULD YOU RATHER:

Have a visible bogey on your nose OR food on your face?

WOULD YOU RATHER:

Lick a clean toilet OR a used shower floor?

WOULD YOU RATHER:

Accidentally show up at a party in fancy dress (no-one else is wearing a costume) OR audibly fart in a lift and everyone know it was you?

WOULD YOU RATHER:

Be able to pee silently OR never need a poo when visiting other people's houses?

WOULD YOU RATHER:

Look good in every photograph OR always smell good?

WOULD YOU RATHER:

Live in eternal darkness OR bright light?

WOULD YOU RATHER:

Be successful in business OR successful in love?

WOULD YOU RATHER:

Use a toothbrush previously used to scrub your bathroom floor OR a toothbrush used to clean a stranger's mouth?

After a long day of playing Pokémon Go and freestyle rap battling you are exhausted and just want to get back to your hotel and relax. Sadly, the budget hotel you booked has had some problems with the booking so looks like your sharing a room! Thankfully the receptionist is feeling generous so you get to pick your roommate. So, would you rather share a room with:

- Rats OR bats?

- Mosquitos OR wasps?

- Scorpions OR snakes?

- A grizzly bear OR lion?

- Your partner's parents OR an alligator?

- Donald Trump OR an elderly nudist?

- An out of tune violinist OR an overflowing toilet?

- Someone throwing up OR someone with diarrhoea?

- Someone with a contagious rash OR angry bull?

- Someone that keeps pinching you OR someone who keeps pulling your hair?

You are going on a date. It's a blind date that your friends have set up for you at a restaurant. You have dressed in your best outfit and feel ready to go, However, on a first date who knows what will happen! So, would you rather your date:

- Has breath like a decomposing badger OR spits when they talk?
- Eats nothing and watches you judgingly as you eat OR steals your food whilst you are in the toilet?
- Talks about nothing but the pros and cons of printer paper OR doesn't talk at all?
- Only refers to themselves in the third person OR shouts when they talk?
- Only talks about their ex OR talks about your future wedding?
- Never makes eye contact OR stares intensely?
- Sings children's theme songs under their breath OR mutters about chasing badgers?
- Takes a sip of your drink and leaves food floaters OR wet sneezes in your food?
- Spends the whole time on Facebook OR continuously goes to the toilet?
- Orders expensive champagne and caviar and then runs out of the restaurant without paying OR throws a bowl of steaming tomato soup into your lap?

You are round your partner's parents' house for Sunday lunch. You get a text from an anonymous number, it reads: "I have taken your (insert most important thing in your life) hostage. If you do not follow my instructions, you will never see it/them again." You must complete ten challenges or else! So as you sit down for lunch would you rather:

- Kick your partners mum in the shins under the table OR pour hot gravy in your lap?
- Loudly say that you are glad there is sweetcorn as you are currently constipated OR drink the whole jug of steaming gravy?
- Eat your dinner like an animal without knife and fork OR start a food fight?
- Take your top off and wave it above your head football fan style OR kiss your partners father?
- Tell everyone that you don't believe in toilet paper and would rather use your hand to wipe OR that the roast dinner tastes worse than the food you ate in prison?
- Rub salt OR pepper into your eyes?
- Tell your partners mother that you hate their home OR that you hate orphans?
- Stand up and freestyle rap "8 Mile" style OR sing opera style?
- Swallow your knife OR fork?
- Smash a plate over your head OR pour custard over your partner?

Humans suck right with all the wars, bullying and lying. Well not on your watch! As self-appointed "Minister for Fairness" it's time to get planet earth sorted. So would you rather stop:

- Bullying OR littering?

- People spitting OR leaving chewing gum on seats?

- Animal cruelty OR ocean pollution?

- People smoking OR speeding?

- Anti-social behaviour OR online trolling?

- Spam emails OR PPI calls?

- The sale of drugs OR guns?

- Tall people standing in front of you at gigs OR people walking slowly in front of you?

- Chefs spitting in food OR people weeing in swimming pools?

- People lying OR stealing?

The big day has arrived. As you make your way to your job interview you are feeling confident and ready to impress. When you sit down though, things begin to change and you start to feel the first prickles of panic. In the words of Dr. Pepper what's the worst that can happen! Would you rather:

- Your CV turns out to be a naked picture of yourself OR the plans for a terrorist plot?

- Audibly poo yourself OR vomit when asked about your strengths?

- Give a presentation and mid-way through realise you are only wearing pants OR that you have been singing the lyrics to Miley Cyrus – Wrecking Ball?

- Look across and realise you are begin interviewed by your ex-partner OR former boss?

- Have every sixth word you say be "stab" OR "Otorhinolaryngologist"?

- Have to perform open heart surgery (you are not a doctor) on your best friend OR defuse a bomb in a puppy Orphanage?

- Only be able to answer questions in the voice of Mr. Burns OR Kermit the Frog?

- Have to tell the interviewer that you once stole their grandma's walking stick OR that you deliberately pushed their child into a pond?

- Have to pick the nose of the interviewer OR pop a spot on their back?

- Shake hands with them after they have just sneezed OR scratched their bare bottom?

WOULD YOU RATHER DOODLE: A collection of hilarious hypothetical questions

Vol:1

- By Clint Hammerstrike

Helpful Guide

To aid you on this journey of self-discovery I have suggested a couple of rules to help you through.

Rule 1: You must answer. Even if you would rather do neither you MUST pick!

Rule 2: Don't rush your answer. Give yourself time to consider the sheer complexity and horror/joy of the choice!

Rule 3: Respect the opinion of those reading with you? Even when they are plainly wrong!

Rule 4: Take this seriously, we are considering the meaning of life do not even consider laughing!

Rule 5: Forget rule 4. Laugh, come on its eating a monkey or kangaroo brain!

Rule 6: Draw whatever it is that you have chosen as your favoured option. How you decide to do this is up to you. Be as creative and detailed as you want. Send your best picture to clinthammerstrike@gmail.com and you could feature in a future edition! Alternatively share it online at: facebook.com/ClintHammerstrike

Let's get drawing

WOULD YOU RATHER:

Fart party poppers OR burp confetti?

___

WOULD YOU RATHER:

Eat a tablespoon of extra extra hot sauce OR get a
brain freeze chugging a slush puppy?

___

WOULD YOU RATHER:

Not give up your seat on a train to a pensioner OR a
pregnant woman?

WOULD YOU RATHER:

Have a hairy nose OR hairy ears?

WOULD YOU RATHER:

Brush your teeth with a squirrel OR a teacup pig?

WOULD YOU RATHER:

Suck on a hiker's socks OR lick a sumo wrestler's nappy?

WOULD YOU RATHER:

Eat someone else's scab OR earwax?

WOULD YOU RATHER:

Rub hot sauce OR vinegar into your eye?

WOULD YOU RATHER:

Be able to make people dance OR sing by shaking their hand?

WOULD YOU RATHER:

Be Superman OR Ironman?

WOULD YOU RATHER:

Go zorbing with a porcupine OR a skunk?

WOULD YOU RATHER:

Be trapped in a lift with a couple kissing OR fighting?

WOULD YOU RATHER:

Climb to the top of Mount Everest OR be Knighted?

WOULD YOU RATHER:

Live in a penthouse suite OR a country cottage?

WOULD YOU RATHER:

Always be sweaty OR itchy?

WOULD YOU RATHER:

Have the trunk of an elephant OR the legs of a giraffe?

WOULD YOU RATHER:

Have a finger for a tongue OR tongues for fingers?

WOULD YOU RATHER:

Eat a rat OR wear it as a necklace?

WOULD YOU RATHER:

Eat a monkey that tastes of cheese OR a llama that tastes of bacon?

WOULD YOU RATHER:

Be the strongest OR the smartest person in the world?

WOULD YOU RATHER:

Juggle lobsters OR hedgehogs?

WOULD YOU RATHER:

Sleep in a bed with spiders OR cockroaches?

WOULD YOU RATHER:

Have a house with 101 cats OR dogs?

WOULD YOU RATHER:

Be a lion tamer OR a trapeze artist?

WOULD YOU RATHER:

Sweat gravy OR custard?

WOULD YOU RATHER:

Have a nose twice as small OR twice as big as normal?

WOULD YOU RATHER:

Your skin has the pattern of a zebra OR a leopard?

WOULD YOU RATHER:

Be able to swim like a dolphin OR climb like a monkey?

WOULD YOU RATHER:

Be lost in the desert OR in the jungle?

WOULD YOU RATHER:

Be able to fly OR be super strong?

WOULD YOU RATHER:

Be Donald Trump OR a human cannon ball?

WOULD YOU RATHER:

Kiss a jellyfish OR a scorpion?

WOULD YOU RATHER:

Dance with King Kong OR Godzilla?

WOULD YOU RATHER:

Be the tallest person in the world OR the shortest?

WOULD YOU RATHER:

Have feet as long as your legs OR legs as long as your feet?

WOULD YOU RATHER:

Be covered in feathers OR fur?

WOULD YOU RATHER:

Lick the back of a stranger knees OR their armpits?

WOULD YOU RATHER:

Live at the South Pole OR North Pole?

WOULD YOU RATHER:

Go back one hundred years into the past OR forward
one hundred years into the future?

WOULD YOU RATHER:

Shower in tea OR coffee?

WOULD YOU RATHER:

Have a dog with a parrot face OR a shark face?

WOULD YOU RATHER:

Greet people by rubbing noses OR bottoms together?

WOULD YOU RATHER:

Go paintballing in a mankini/bikini OR a hospital gown?

WOULD YOU RATHER:

Eat a deep fried Mars Bar OR a doughnut burger?

WOULD YOU RATHER:

Re-take your High School exams OR have major
dental work?

WOULD YOU RATHER:

Have the face of a Panda OR a lion?

WOULD YOU RATHER:

Cook dinner for the Queen of England OR the President of the USA?

WOULD YOU RATHER:

Tightrope walk across the Grand Canyon holding a snake OR a scorpion?

WOULD YOU RATHER:

Spend the day with a crab OR a Gecko in your underwear?

WOULD YOU RATHER:

Run a marathon carrying a fridge OR without any trainers?

WOULD YOU RATHER:

Have an office job OR work outside?

_____

WOULD YOU RATHER:

Be a tree OR a flower?

_____

WOULD YOU RATHER:

Spend a day in the life of a movie star OR Rock/Pop star?

___

WOULD YOU RATHER:

Get married and discover you partner was an assassin OR has a secret family?

___

WOULD YOU RATHER:

Be a skilled archer OR sword fighter?

_____

WOULD YOU RATHER:

Be a Samurai or a Medieval Knight?

_____

WOULD YOU RATHER:

Never be able to use a knife OR a fork again?

WOULD YOU RATHER:

Have to drink out of your shoe OR a stranger's motorcycle helmet?

WOULD YOU RATHER:

Have a lightsabre OR a hover board (one that actually hovers not a rubbish one with wheels)?

WOULD YOU RATHER:

Be a contestant in "The Hunger Games" OR be a gladiator in ancient Rome?

WOULD YOU RATHER:

Be pursued by Zombie Koalas OR Wereblobfishes
(werewolf + blob fish hybrid)?

___

WOULD YOU RATHER:

Have to wear a sombrero OR a Hawaiian shirt for the
rest of your life?

___

WOULD YOU RATHER:

Have a bird's nest OR a squirrel's drey (nest) in your hair?

___

WOULD YOU RATHER:

Be an airplane pilot OR a boat captain?

___

WOULD YOU RATHER:

Drink 10 pints of your own urine OR 1 pint of someone else's?

WOULD YOU RATHER:

Be able to do a handstand OR a cartwheel?

WOULD YOU RATHER:

Eat cabbage OR cauliflower for every meal
(including breakfast) for the rest of your life?

WOULD YOU RATHER:

Have a colonic irrigation OR give someone else one?

WOULD YOU RATHER:

Be a sloth OR a tiger?

WOULD YOU RATHER:

Poo OR vomit every time someone says your name?

WOULD YOU RATHER:

Be able to turn invisible OR move things with your mind?

WOULD YOU RATHER:

Eat a tub or butter OR a 6 pack of eggs raw?

WOULD YOU RATHER:

Be punched by a gorilla OR kicked by a kangaroo?

WOULD YOU RATHER:

Wear a leotard OR a wedding dress for the rest of your life?

WOULD YOU RATHER:

Wear clown make up or goth make up for the rest of your life?

WOULD YOU RATHER:

Hit the game winning home run OR throw the game winning pitch?

WOULD YOU RATHER:

Be a mermaid/man OR a unicorn?

WOULD YOU RATHER:

Be a cat OR a dog?

WOULD YOU RATHER:

Be able to juggle OR ride a unicycle?

WOULD YOU RATHER:

Have a tattoo of a lobster wearing a tuxedo OR a tortoise playing a banjo?

WOULD YOU RATHER:

Be an artist or an author?

WOULD YOU RATHER:

Be raised by lions OR monkeys?

WOULD YOU RATHER:

Always have smelly fish OR smelly cheese in your pocket?

WOULD YOU RATHER:

Have a third arm growing out of your head OR your stomach?

WOULD YOU RATHER:

Be able to transform into a penguin OR a meerkat?

WOULD YOU RATHER:

Fight 1 brown bear OR 30 Lemurs?

WOULD YOU RATHER:

Be a chef OR a florist?

WOULD YOU RATHER:

Have a unicorn horn or a halo on your head?

WOULD YOU RATHER:

Lick a shower floor OR the gap in-between
someone's toes?

WOULD YOU RATHER:

Take a bath with an alligator OR a shark?

WOULD YOU RATHER:

Be a contortionist OR a magician?

WOULD YOU RATHER:

Every time you sneeze a parrot OR a puppy comes out?

WOULD YOU RATHER:

Be able to poop out burgers OR pizza?

WOULD YOU RATHER:

Have chocolate bars for fingers OR crème eggs for eyes?

WOULD YOU RATHER:

Live in a house made of chocolate OR cake?

WOULD YOU RATHER:

Wear a toga OR a Pokémon onesie to a job interview?

WOULD YOU RATHER:

Be a detective OR a doctor?

WOULD YOU RATHER:

Skydive OR bungee jump?

WOULD YOU RATHER:

Be trapped in space for a year on your own OR with a person you hate?

WOULD YOU RATHER:

Eat your bodyweight in earwax or Bogeys?

WOULD YOU RATHER DOODLE: A collection of hilarious hypothetical questions

Vol:2

- By Clint Hammerstrike

Let's get drawing

WOULD YOU RATHER:

Wear a snake as a tie OR a rat as a bow tie?

WOULD YOU RATHER:

Burp out wasps OR mosquitos?

WOULD YOU RATHER:

Collect door knobs OR corkscrews?

WOULD YOU RATHER:

Collect takeaway serviettes OR bottle tops?

WOULD YOU RATHER:

Look good from close up, but ugly from far away OR look good from far away, but ugly close up?

WOULD YOU RATHER:

Be stuck on a rollercoaster with a porcupine OR a skunk?

WOULD YOU RATHER:

Never have to pay tax again OR have a six pack?

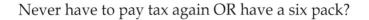

WOULD YOU RATHER:

Chop a frostbitten toe off with a spoon OR a fountain pen?

WOULD YOU RATHER:

Collect other people's scabs OR dried bogies?

WOULD YOU RATHER:

Go skydiving naked or bungee jumping naked?

WOULD YOU RATHER:

Be followed around by a herd of unicorns OR
dragons?

WOULD YOU RATHER:

Eat your body weight in candy floss OR skittles?

WOULD YOU RATHER:

Carry 10 crabs OR 10 mice in your pants for a day?

WOULD YOU RATHER:

Wear a suit made from tin foil OR bubble-wrap?

WOULD YOU RATHER:

Be followed around by a Mariachi (traditional Mexican) band OR a brass marching band?

WOULD YOU RATHER:

Fly a helicopter with an angry badger OR a swarm of bees for co-pilot?

WOULD YOU RATHER:

Have the face of a sloth OR a koala?

WOULD YOU RATHER:

Eat a jar of mayonnaise OR marmite?

WOULD YOU RATHER:

Go streaking at a Royal wedding OR the 100m
Olympic final?

WOULD YOU RATHER:

Use a towel after a sweaty person has used it OR
wear someone else's retainer?

WOULD YOU RATHER:

Be able to control the weather OR people's moods?

WOULD YOU RATHER:

Have a key that opens any door OR access to anybody's phone number?

WOULD YOU RATHER:

Be able to breathe under water OR never be too hot or cold?

WOULD YOU RATHER:

Always hear banjo music OR bagpipes?

WOULD YOU RATHER:

Go speed dating wearing a rabbit onesie OR a spandex leotard?

WOULD YOU RATHER:

Go for a night out with Bruce Banner OR the Hulk?

WOULD YOU RATHER:

Fight off a sword wielding pirate with a guitar
OR a trumpet?

WOULD YOU RATHER:

Play football wearing scuba flippers OR high
heels?

WOULD YOU RATHER:

Replace your arms with octopi's tentacles OR
lobster claws?

WOULD YOU RATHER:

Be able to live everyday once over OR twice a
day be able to rewind time by one hour?

WOULD YOU RATHER:

Eat a spikey cactus OR a llama's eyeball?

WOULD YOU RATHER:

Have a contactless payment chip installed in your hand so you could buy things with a fist bump OR high-5?

WOULD YOU RATHER:

Drink tea through your ears OR belly-button?

WOULD YOU RATHER:

Always wear hot pants OR an orange boiler suit?

WOULD YOU RATHER:

Eat a doughnut covered in mayonnaise OR mustard?

WOULD YOU RATHER:

Shower in pesto OR cheese sauce?

WOULD YOU RATHER:

Drink a pint of Brussel sprout smoothie OR
Sushi smoothie?

WOULD YOU RATHER:

Eat a large pine cone OR be a human dart board and have three darts thrown at you?

WOULD YOU RATHER:

Kiss a camel OR a snake?

WOULD YOU RATHER:

Ride a camel across a desert OR drive huskies
and sled across the arctic?

WOULD YOU RATHER:

Have the horns of a bull OR feet of a duck?

WOULD YOU RATHER:

Sing the national anthem every time you eat OR drink?

WOULD YOU RATHER:

Bath in melted cheese or melted chocolate?

WOULD YOU RATHER:

Live a day as a kangaroo or a killer-whale?

WOULD YOU RATHER:

Everyone look like Donald Trump OR Scooby-Do?

WOULD YOU RATHER:

Never be sad again OR never feel physical pain again?

WOULD YOU RATHER:

Put a nappy on a grizzly bear or a lion?

WOULD YOU RATHER:

Be able to remember everything you ever read
OR be able run the 100m in 9.4 seconds?

WOULD YOU RATHER:

Have a pet dinosaur OR dragon?

WOULD YOU RATHER:

Win Wimbledon OR the Superbowl?

WOULD YOU RATHER:

Live a day in the life of Homer Simpson or Peter Griffin?

WOULD YOU RATHER:

Spend the day looking after a meerkat or a
teacup pig?

WOULD YOU RATHER:

Never have to sleep again OR never have to use
the toilet again?

WOULD YOU RATHER:

Have sunflowers OR roses growing out of your ears?

WOULD YOU RATHER:

Fry bacon naked OR go on a bouncy castle with a cup of tea?

WOULD YOU RATHER:

Be a football (soccer) star OR a basketball star?

WOULD YOU RATHER:

Spend a day shopping OR chilling by the beach?

WOULD YOU RATHER:

Eat monkey OR kangaroo brain?

WOULD YOU RATHER:

Drive a monster truck OR a Ferrari?

WOULD YOU RATHER:

Live in a treehouse OR a yurt?

WOULD YOU RATHER:

All men looked like rhinos OR all women look like penguins?

WOULD YOU RATHER:

Have an elephant or hippo sneeze in your mouth
while you yawn?

WOULD YOU RATHER:

All babies look like doughnuts OR all pensioners
look like pretzels?

WOULD YOU RATHER:

Be pushed down a waterfall riding in a barrel
OR on an inflatable unicorn?

WOULD YOU RATHER:

Have ten good friends OR two great friends?

WOULD YOU RATHER:

Be able to stretch and put your feet behind your ears OR be able to punch through a tree?

WOULD YOU RATHER:

Eat a plate of dry skin flakes OR belly button fluff?

WOULD YOU RATHER:

Have all your thoughts appear in a speech bubble above your head OR wear your underwear on the outside?

WOULD YOU RATHER:

Eat nothing but steak OR bread for a month?

WOULD YOU RATHER:

Be caught up in a Sharknado (Tornado plus sharks!) OR be given a rectal exam by Wolverine?

WOULD YOU RATHER:

Eat the board game Monopoly OR have a picture of you pooing sent to everyone in your phone's contact list?

WOULD YOU RATHER:

Every photo of you looks like Ronald McDonald
OR Colonel Sanders?

WOULD YOU RATHER:

Be given a massage by Donald Trump OR
Vladimir Putin?

WOULD YOU RATHER:

Have a tattoo for every poo you have ever taken
OR a tattoo for every swear word you have ever
said?

WOULD YOU RATHER:

Whilst on a rocking boat Tattoo a picture of a
giraffe onto the eyelid OR tongue of a friend?

WOULD YOU RATHER:

Have your hair cut by an 8-year-old OR have
them pick all your clothes for three months?

WOULD YOU RATHER:

Every time you lie your nose shrinks (reverse
Pinocchio) OR your fingers get longer?

WOULD YOU RATHER:

Be born knowing everything that will ever happen to you OR live life as an adventure not knowing your future?

WOULD YOU RATHER:

Never read a book OR never hear music again?

WOULD YOU RATHER:

Randomly once a day turn into Elmo or Kermit the frog?

WOULD YOU RATHER:

Would you rather fight Papa Smurf OR Winnie the Pooh?

WOULD YOU RATHER:

Travel to work by pedalo OR bumpercar?

WOULD YOU RATHER:

Be chauffeur driven in a milk float OR a cycle rickshaw?

WOULD YOU RATHER:

Have one pair of underwear OR one tissue for whole year?

WOULD YOU RATHER:

Pay for all your purchases by singing or dancing?

WOULD YOU RATHER:

Eat unicorn (rainbow coloured ice-cream) poop
OR dragon (cheese and jalapeno nacho) poop?

WOULD YOU RATHER:

Win an Olympic Gold medal OR a Nobel Prize?

WOULD YOU RATHER:

Have to eat your way out of a room full of
Krispy Kreme donuts OR chocolate fudge cake?

WOULD YOU RATHER:

Have to eat your bodyweight in Stuffed Crust
Pizzas OR Cheeseburgers?

WOULD YOU RATHER:

Use peanut butter OR hummus as toothpaste for a week?

WOULD YOU RATHER:

Be a world class pole-vaulter OR poet?

WOULD YOU RATHER:

Be able to teleport OR travel back in time?

WOULD YOU RATHER:

Go to a fancy ball wearing a chicken onesie OR a space suit?

WOULD YOU RATHER:

Greet the Queen with an Eskimo kiss OR a fist bump?

WOULD YOU RATHER:

Live in a house haunted by a rap battling OR bagpipe playing ghost?

WOULD YOU RATHER:

Read every fiction book OR see every film?

WOULD YOU RATHER:

Be the world's greatest poker OR chess player?

WOULD YOU RATHER:

Be able to answer all general knowledge questions OR be a mathematics genius?

WOULD YOU RATHER:

Live in snow-capped mountains OR by the beach?

WOULD YOU RATHER:

Spend a week living as an astronaut OR as Sherlock Holmes (Benedict Cumberbatch style Sherlock)?

WOULD YOU RATHER SURVIVAL: A collection of hilarious hypothetical questions

- By Clint Hammerstrike

Chapter 1: Shipwreck Survivor!

Scenario:

Is there anything better than a cruise through the tropical paradise of the South Pacific? Unfortunately for you the cruise ship captain has taken a wrong turn somewhere off the Island of Fiji. You are now shipwrecked with little chance of survival! Fortunately, you have been marooned with a diverse range of people but the island is only big enough to support 11. Guess it's time to start choosing your survival crew. Your survival will depend on them. So . . . . .

Would you rather team up with:

Antony McPartlin OR Declan Donnelly?

Arnold Schwarzenegger OR Sylvester Stallone?

James Bond OR Jason Bourne?

Homer Simpson OR Peter Griffin?

Donald Trump OR Vladimir Putin?

Katniss Everdeen OR Rey?

Cast of Friends: Chandler, Joey, Monica, Phoebe, Rachel OR Ross (choose one)?

Jon Snow OR Daenerys Targaryen?

Ironman OR Captain America?

Pooh Bear OR Tigger?

Chapter 2: Emergency Fallout Shelter!

<u>Scenario:</u>

He only went and pushed the red button with those tiny hands of his! Now you are going to be stuck in an underground emergency shelter on your own for the next three years whilst you sit out the worst of it. The only problem is that you didn't stock up very well. Still, in the last few minutes before you close the hatch you have time to make some last minute choices. Choose wisely it is going to be a rough few years. So . . . . . .

What would you have as your:

One movie?

One TV boxset?

Three luxury toiletries?

One luxury food item (in addition to basic rations)?

One luxury drink (to supplement water)?

One book?

One album?

One conversation with a famous person for 30 minutes to be used at any time?

One personal item?

One pet?

Chapter 3: Anarchy!

<u>Scenario:</u>

The uprising has taken place, anarchy has overthrown the powers that be and you have been appointed world leader! Taking your place on your plush new throne you are asked to pass verdict on the most pressing issues of dystopian society. Think carefully the fate of the world depends on you. Make the wrong choice and there could be an angry mob around the corner! So . . . . . .

Would you rather:

Save the chocolate OR doughnut production factory?

Would you rather:

Save the crisps OR biscuit production factory?

Would you rather:

Save the alcohol OR toilet paper production factory?

Would you rather:

Save the last remaining boxset of TV Show "Friends" OR "Big Bang Theory"?

Would you rather:

Save cats OR dogs from extinction?

Would you rather:

Have working toilets OR working televisions?

Would you rather:

Have clothes OR beds?

Would you rather:

Have music OR meat?

Would you rather:

Have everyone greet you by high five OR fist bump?

Would you rather:

Have everyone tattooed on their forehead with a skateboarding badger OR a breakdancing porcupine?

Chapter 4: Zombie Koala Rising!

Scenario:

It's happened, we always expected that it might. Zombie Koala's have risen and are slowly chomping their way through the human race. Every time a person is bitten they transform into a monstrously cute Zombie Koala. Nowhere is safe and who knows who you can trust. If you are going to make it through to safety you are going to have to choose wisely so . . . . . .

Would you rather:

Use a 5-year-old OR an old age pensioner as a weapon?

Would you rather:

Use puppies OR kittens as body armour?

Would you rather:

Use your mother OR your partner as a distraction to escape?

Would you rather:

Loot a toy store OR a beauty salon for supplies?

Would you rather:

Team up with a band of Morris dancers OR Bell ringers?

Would you rather:

Hideout in an overflowing public toilet OR a container ship filled with rotting fish?

Would you rather:

Save a class of children from a viciously cute koala attack OR leave them to their fate and find a shotgun with plenty of ammo?

Would you rather:

Drink water filtered through a stranger's pants OR your own used toilet paper?

Would you rather:

Eat a non-zombie Koala raw OR a Zombie Koala cooked?

Would you rather:

Be the last human alive for eternity OR give up and join the Zombie Koalas?

Chapter 5: Jungle Madness!

Scenario:
Is there a better way to pass a lazy Tuesday afternoon then taking a stroll through the Amazon? For you the answer is yes. Were you supposed to take the second left or first right after passing the river? Distracted by all that machete hacking you have chosen poorly and are now lost in the jungle! As sweat pours down your face and insects crawl up your leg it's time to survive so . . . . . .

Would you rather:

Sacrifice your trousers OR shirt to stop a nasty cut getting infected?

Would you rather:

Drink a pint of your own urine OR drink from a puddle with a dead rodent next to it?

Would you rather:

Eat a snake OR monkey raw?

Would you rather:

Sleep near a snake pit OR scorpion nest?

Would you rather:

Wade across a river that may have crocodiles in it OR walk for an extra day through dense jungle to find a bridge?

Would you rather:

Sacrifice your knife OR your torch to escape a Tiger attack?

Would you rather:

Spend the night in a cave OR in the branches of a tree?

Would you rather:

Stop mosquitos biting your face by covering yourself with yesterday's pants OR socks?

Would you rather:

Filter water through yesterday's socks OR pants?

Would you rather:

Sacrifice your last pair of clean pants OR socks to start a fire?

Chapter 6: Mountain Escape!

<u>Scenario:</u>

The climb up was so easy. Who would have thought that coming down the mountain would be so difficult? Turns out that texting whilst mountain climbing is a really bad idea. It looks like you have a suspected broken leg so it could be a long couple of days. Getting off this mountain in one piece is going to take all your wits. So as you wince with the pain . . . . . .

Would you rather:

Share your tent with a porcupine OR a skunk?

Would you rather:

Lose your map OR your phone?

Would you rather:

Lose your painkillers OR your torch?

Would you rather:

Eat raw spiders OR worms?

Would you rather:

It is raining and you have no coat OR its roasting and you have no hat/sun cream?

Would you rather:

Have no clothes just walking boots OR clothes but no walking boots?

Would you rather:

Be guided down the mountain by a hallucination of Yoda OR Bear Grylls?

Would you rather:

Eat yellow snow OR go thirsty?

Would you rather:

Have wet socks OR a constant wedgie?

Would you rather:

Use the last of your fuel to cook dinner OR heat your tent through a cold night?

Chapter 7: Desert Despair!

Scenario:

You decided to take your private jet out for a quick flight over the desert. As you take in the endless miles of sand dunes you hear an alarm sounding. Shame you forgot to fill up the tank with fuel! Now you are going to have to jump out or perform an emergency landing. So, as you begin to lose altitude . . . . . .

Would you rather:

Attempt to land the plane OR parachute out?

Would you rather:

Use an umbrella OR a bedsheet as a parachute?

Would you rather:

Parachute down and land on a cluster of prickly cacti OR boulders?

Would you rather:

Quickly grab a phone OR a bottle of water?

Would you rather:

Quickly grab a hat OR a map?

Would you rather:

Quickly grab a first aid kit OR a bag of snack sized Mars bars?

Would you rather:

Call air traffic control but only be able to communicate by singing OR rapping?

Would you rather:

Make a quick phone call to Donald Trump OR Kim Jong-Un?

Would you rather:

Be instructed how to land the plane by a sober 8-year old OR a drunk 35-year-old?

Would you rather:

Land the plane in quick sand OR a pit of angry poisonous snakes?

Chapter 8: Scavenger Hunt!

Scenario:

Adventurers, scavenging rats and the contestants on come dine with me - what have they all got in common? The answer is they will eat anything! Your stomach begins to rumble and it has been a while since you last ate. As the last person on Earth it looks like you are going to have to compromise on flavour. Scavenging for food can lead to some creative culinary choices so . . . . . .

Would you rather eat:

A magpie OR a crow?

Would you rather eat:

Roasted rat OR pan fried pigeon?

Would you rather eat:

Slugs OR snails?

Would you rather eat:

Expired yoghurt OR expired feta cheese?

Would you rather eat:

A half-eaten Beef Burger OR half-eaten Pizza?

Would you rather eat:

Boiled Cauliflower OR Cabbage?

Would you rather eat:

Dairy Milk chocolate OR Galaxy chocolate?

Would you rather eat:

Dry Shredded Wheat OR dry Weetabix?

Would you rather eat:

Baked badger OR fried fox?

Would you rather eat:

Fresh caught rabbit OR fish?

Chapter 9: Alone in London!

Scenario:

"All by myself, don't want to be, all by myself anymore". Celine Dion knew was she was doing when she wrote that song. Too bad for you that you are the last person on Earth, stuck in central London with plenty of time on your hands. The good news is that London is your playground and nothing is off-limits! No queueing for entry, no getting turned away for wearing trainers and no security telling you "don't touch that"! So with London at your mercy . . . . . .

Would you rather:

Make Buckingham Palace OR No.10 Downing Street your home?

Would you rather:

Go shopping for free in Harrods OR Fortnum and Mason?

Would you rather:

Streak through Bond Street OR Hyde Park?

Would you rather:

Stay at the Ritz OR the Savoy hotel?

Would you rather:

Drive a train OR a double decker bus?

Would you rather:

Use the toilets in the House of Commons OR Windsor Castle?

Would you rather:

Grab a sharpie and go to the wax works at Madam Tussauds OR the national portrait gallery?

Would you rather:

Free all the animals in London Zoo OR save them for future dinners?

Would you rather:

Dance at the Royal Opera house OR Sing on the West End?

Would you rather:

Climb to the top of the Millennium Wheel OR the Shard?

Chapter 10: Christmas Chaos!

Scenario:

How could they do it. Up and leave you on your own at Christmas for the holidays. Still, it's not the first time this has happened and by now you know the drill. But with pesky robbers looking to steal your mediocre laptop and prize collection of Happy Meal toys it's time to prepare. This is your house; you have to defend it! So with home defence on your mind . . . . . .

How would you defend:

The garden?

How would you defend:

The front door?

How would you defend:

The back Door?

How would you defend:

The ground floor windows?

How would you defend:

The first floor windows?

How would you defend:

The hallway?

How would you defend:

The TV room?

How would you defend:

The Kitchen?

How would you defend:

The Bathroom?

How would you defend:

The Bedrooms?

Chapter 11: Lucky Looting!

Scenario:

Surviving alone in an urban waste land is no picnic. How you would love to be tucking into a picnic mmmm sausage rolls! Still the upside is that everything is free. Is it looting if there is no-one to actually be taking it from. Plenty of time to ponder that moral question later. Now it is all about surviving, such a shame there is a limit to what you can carry. How you choose to survive will influence what you will need to guarantee your survival. So, to boost your survival chances . . . . . .

Would you rather take:

Solar panels OR a Diesel Generator?

Would you rather take:

A first aid kit OR a how-to medical guide?

Would you rather take:

A lighter OR a torch?

Would you rather take:

An axe OR a knife?

Would you rather take:

A tent OR a sleeping bag?

Would you rather take:

Walking boots OR a big coat?

Would you rather take:

A camping stove OR a water bottle?

Would you rather take:

A map OR a compass?

Would you rather take:

Energy bars OR water?

Would you rather take:

A bow and arrows OR a crossbow?

Chapter 12: Creature comforts!

Sweet electricity! Turns out that it really is useful. Wild camping in the middle of nowhere has its benefits (less Zombie Koalas, riots and bandits) but surviving without creature comforts is a real pain. As you cry yourself to sleep knowing that your laptop is now out of battery (no more Netflix for you) . . . . . .

Which would you miss more:

A fridge OR a freezer?

Which would you miss more:

An oven OR a microwave?

Which would you miss more:

A smartphone OR a laptop?

Which would you miss more:

A bath OR a shower?

Which would you miss more:

A toothbrush OR a razor?

Which would you miss more:

Running water OR central heating?

Which would you miss more:

YouTube OR Facebook?

Which would you miss more:

Instagram OR Twitter?

Which would you miss more:

A sofa OR a bed?

Which would you miss more:

Netflix OR Amazon Prime?

Chapter 13: Cold Shoulder!

Scenario:

Thank goodness you wore that second pair of pants. Turns out the Arctic is one cold place to drive a sled with huskies – it's no wonder Santa Claus has a beard and a belly! Unfortunately for you, trying to do doughnuts you have gone and broken your sled. Now you are stuck in the middle of nowhere with limited supplies! Surviving here is going to take some survival skills and determination so . . . . . .

Would you rather:

Eat one of your huskies OR go hungry and feed the weakest husky to the pack to keep them strong?

Would you rather:

Use parts from your sled to make a shelter OR a signal fire?

Would you rather:

Eat your emergency food straight away OR try and ration them out?

Would you rather:

Use the last of your fuel for melting snow for water OR for keeping warm?

Would you rather:

Wear your bright orange coat OR use it as a flag to attract attention?

Would you rather:

Use your urine OR poo to create a large S.O.S message?

Would you rather:

Try and catch a polar bear OR killer whale to eat?

Would you rather:

Eat a seal raw OR go hungry?

Would you rather:

Drink your own urine OR go thirsty?

Would you rather:

Keep your survival guide OR use it to start a fire (it's your only kindling item left)?

Chapter 14: Re-building Society!

<u>Scenario</u>

Being a survivor can't be all fun and games. Sometimes you have to get down to the nitty gritty or re-building the world as we know it. As you know it's not what you know but who you know that counts! Who needs to know how to fix a toilet, build a house or perform brain surgery when you can either Google "How to ……" or find the details of someone that can do the job. Well in a post-Google society it is time to make some choices about who you want to know. It's time to pick your dream team so ……

Would you rather:

A plumber OR an electrician?

Would you rather:

A farmer OR a doctor?

Would you rather:

A judge OR a policeman/woman?

Would you rather:

An architect OR a builder?

Would you rather:

A veterinarian OR a butcher?

Would you rather:

A baker OR a hunter?

Would you rather:

A singer OR an author?

Would you rather:

A soldier OR a nurse?

Would you rather:

A pilot OR a ship captain?

Would you rather:

A clothes maker OR shoe maker?

Chapter 15: Water weirdness!

<u>Scenario</u>

Living the life of the rich and famous certainly has its upsides. As you sun yourself on the expensive yacht you borrowed from your millionaire mate your troubles just drift away. Unfortunately for you the dark clouds on the horizon are drifting towards you at the same time. As the storm begins to rage and your stomach turns, it is time to batten down the hatches and get ready to bail so . . . . . .

Would you rather:

Use an inflatable unicorn OR flamingo as a flotation aid?

Would you rather:

Use a colander OR a wire trash can to bail out seawater?

Would you rather:

Let Jack climb onto your large piece of ship wreckage OR be selfish and leave him in the water? See Titanic for the wrong answer!

Would you rather:

Fight an octopus OR a hammerhead shark?

Would you rather:

Be seasick overboard and everybody know OR swallow your vomit back down and no-body know?

Would you rather:

Share a lifeboat with a tiger OR a gorilla?

Would you rather:

As the ship lurches, stitch up a large cut on your crewmate cheek OR remove a crewmates tooth?

Would you rather:

As the ship lurches, carry a tray of boiling hot soup OR whale urine samples?

Would you rather:

Have your boat circled by sharks OR piranhas?

Would you rather:

Eat a starfish OR a seahorse?

WOULD YOU RATHER REVOLUTION: A collection of outrageous hypothetical questions

- By Clint Hammerstrike

Let's get drawing

WOULD YOU RATHER:

Take a poo in the toilet of a fancy restaurant
and have to wipe up with your underwear
OR socks?

WOULD YOU RATHER:

Wake up naked in an art gallery OR a
supermarket?

WOULD YOU RATHER:

Live in a house with no roof OR in a house with no walls?

WOULD YOU RATHER:

Always feel like you need to pee OR poo?

WOULD YOU RATHER:

Be rich but never be able to go outside OR poor and be able to go where you like?

WOULD YOU RATHER:

Be a part of the Avengers OR X-Men?

WOULD YOU RATHER:

Have a giant unibrow OR have hair sticking out of your nose and ears?

WOULD YOU RATHER:

Count every star in the sky or every tree in the Amazon?

WOULD YOU RATHER:

Be hunted by Ninja's or the Mafia?

WOULD YOU RATHER:

Eat only hummus and carrots OR have to
walk with crutches for the rest of your life?

WOULD YOU RATHER:

Never be able to wear shoes OR underwear?

WOULD YOU RATHER:

Use a koala OR an owl as a towel?

WOULD YOU RATHER:

Swim the length of a swimming pool filled
with blister fluid OR runny snot?

WOULD YOU RATHER:

Have an IQ of 160 (the same as Stephen
Hawking) or £160 million?

WOULD YOU RATHER:

Be able to restart your life OR continue it as is?

WOULD YOU RATHER:

Be able to talk your way out OR fight your way out of any problematic scenario?

WOULD YOU RATHER:

Lick every object you see OR be licked by everyone that see's you?

WOULD YOU RATHER:

Smell like a skunk OR look like a skunk?

WOULD YOU RATHER:

Have a head the size of an exercise ball OR a satsuma?

WOULD YOU RATHER:

Live in a tree-house OR a cave?

WOULD YOU RATHER:

Lose your sense of smell or taste?

WOULD YOU RATHER:

Be completely bald all over OR hairy all over?

WOULD YOU RATHER:

For a day be accompanied everywhere you go by a naked sumo wrestler OR spend the day dressed as a sumo wrestler?

WOULD YOU RATHER:

All the food you ever eat is free OR all the food you ever eat is calorie free?

WOULD YOU RATHER:

Fight a skinny sumo wrestler OR a lazy
ninja?

WOULD YOU RATHER:

Have no knees OR elbows?

WOULD YOU RATHER:

Have a pet unicorn OR be a unicorn?

WOULD YOU RATHER:

Accidentally share on Facebook a photo of
you on the toilet OR eat a smoothie made of
all the gunk in your shower plug?

WOULD YOU RATHER:

Never be able to smile OR never be able to laugh?

WOULD YOU RATHER:

Lose all the photos you have ever taken OR all the music you have ever owned?

WOULD YOU RATHER:

Be able to pick the next leader of your
country OR invent one new law?

WOULD YOU RATHER:

Would you rather erase all trace of yourself
from the internet OR have the most social
media followers in the world?

WOULD YOU RATHER:

Be able to record everything you see OR
everything you hear?

WOULD YOU RATHER:

Fight Ronald McDonald, Colonel Sander OR
the Burger King?

WOULD YOU RATHER:

Hollywood made a film about your life OR
your favourite band wrote a song about you?

WOULD YOU RATHER:

Give Godzilla a colonic irrigation OR eat a
dozen penguins?

WOULD YOU RATHER:

Write great songs and not be appreciated OR
write terrible songs and be popular?

_____

WOULD YOU RATHER:

Find your soul mate OR a suitcase of cash
that never runs out?

_____

WOULD YOU RATHER:

Find out that your parents are aliens OR
marry your cousin?

WOULD YOU RATHER:

Break your arm surfing OR your leg skiing?

WOULD YOU RATHER:

Spend a night alone in a creepy house in the woods OR in the White House with Donald Trump?

WOULD YOU RATHER:

Be trapped in a lift with the first person you ever kissed OR your ex's mum?

WOULD YOU RATHER:

Run a marathon but on reaching the finishing
line be told you have to run another 5 miles
OR snog a bulldog?

WOULD YOU RATHER:

Have to walk bare foot across a room
covered in slugs OR snails?

WOULD YOU RATHER:

Rub salt OR Lime Juice into a paper cut?

WOULD YOU RATHER:

Be kicked in the shins by a horse OR in the head by a karate instructor?

WOULD YOU RATHER:

Have to stop a nosebleed using a stranger's pants OR their snotty tissue?

WOULD YOU RATHER:

Eskimo kiss your boss OR a pug that has just licked it's bottom?

Working 9 to 5

WOULD YOU RATHER:

Work as a proctologist (anus doctor) OR as a
crime scene cleaner?

_____

WOULD YOU RATHER:

Work as an animal pee collector (yes that is a
real thing) OR as a manure inspector?

_____

WOULD YOU RATHER:

Work as a theme park vomit cleaner (Thorpe Park has one) OR as an odour judge (judging how good and bad things smell)?

WOULD YOU RATHER:

Work as a medical waste disposal worker (think limbs, needles and bandages) OR as a mortician?

WOULD YOU RATHER:

Work as a sewer cleaner OR as a colonic irrigator?

_____

WOULD YOU RATHER:

Work as a maggot farmer OR as a chicken sexer (they determine whether a chicken is a male or female)?

_____

WOULD YOU RATHER:

Work as an Esthetician (includes removing puss from people's spots as they give facial treatments) OR as a slaughterhouse worker?

WOULD YOU RATHER:

Work as a whale snot collector (yes its real, and yes it's as disgusting as advertised) OR as a guano collector (fancy term for someone that collects bat and bird poop)?

WOULD YOU RATHER:

Work as a festival portaloo cleaner OR as a poop stirrer (prepare specimens for DNA testing by stirring to form a suitable solution)?

WOULD YOU RATHER:

Work as a roadkill collector (fox, badger or squirrel get your spade out) OR as an armpit sniffer (how else can deodorant companies know they are doing a good job)?

WOULD YOU RATHER:

Work as a lift pump unblocker (they work at sewerage treatment plants and have to wear full scuba gear to swim through excrement to unblock sewerage pumps) OR as a cavity searcher at a maximum security prison?

WOULD YOU RATHER:

Work as a noodler (catching Catfish by getting them to bite your arm) OR a high rise window cleaner (hope you have a head for heights)?

WOULD YOU RATHER:

Work as a rodeo clown (brought in to distract the very angry bull - good chance you are going to get a kicking) OR a clinical trial subject (let's hope you are in the placebo group)?

WOULD YOU RATHER:

Work as an Alaskan crab fisherman (mortality rate 80% higher than average worker, days without showering and 48 hour straight shifts in freezing conditions) OR as a Hurricane Pilot (NASA wants to understand how hurricanes work so they have pilots who fly through them, yup real!)?

WOULD YOU RATHER:

Work as a skydiving instructor (leaping from a plane – fine, leaping from a plane with a stranger strapped to your chest who could freak out at any time – not fine) OR as a drying paint watcher (not just an expression some people are actually employed to test how long it takes for paints to dry)?

WOULD YOU RATHER:

Work as a train pusher (in Japan Oshiyas are paid to help cram people onto train carriages by shoving them in like Sardines in a tin) OR as a dog food taster (chowing down like a hound, testing new dog food products for flavour and texture)?

WOULD YOU RATHER:

Work as a snake milker (the collector of highly poisonous venom from angry snakes) OR as a naked life art model (yup, just a room full of strangers painting you in all your glory)?

WOULD YOU RATHER:

Work as a professional queuer (some rich dudes going to pay you to stand in line) OR as a golf ball diver (someone needs to collect all those balls you have hooked off the tea)?

WOULD YOU RATHER:

Work as a bed warmer (some Hotels pay
people to wear sleep suits and act as hot
water bottles until guests arrive) OR as a
waterslide tester (as advertised, let's hope
they built it right)?

WOULD YOU RATHER:

Work as a professional bridesmaid (fit in the
dress – you get the job) OR as a professional
mourner (cry on demand – you get the job)?

WOULD YOU RATHER:

Work as a Panda nanny (spending 365 days caring for Panda cubs) OR as a professional foreigner (some Chinese companies will pay big bucks for you to dress up and attend functions)?

WOULD YOU RATHER:

Work as a face feeler (also known as Sensory Scientists who use their hands to judge the effectiveness of lotions) OR as a professional cuddler (not sure if you are the big spoon or little spoon)?

Fear and Phobias

WOULD YOU RATHER:

Suffer from Xanthophobia (a fear of anything yellow - including the sun) OR Porphyrophobia (a fear of anything purple)?

WOULD YOU RATHER:

Suffer from Turophobia (a fear of cheese) OR Hylophobia (a fear of trees)?

WOULD YOU RATHER:

Suffer from Omphalophobia (a fear of the navel) OR Nomophobia (a fear of being without mobile phone coverage)?

WOULD YOU RATHER:

Suffer from Ombrophobia (a fear of rain) OR Pogonophobia (a fear of beards)?

WOULD YOU RATHER:

Suffer from Chionophobia (a fear of snow) OR Ancraophobia (a fear of wind)?

WOULD YOU RATHER:

Suffer from Dextrophobia (a fear of objects being to their right) OR Papyrophobia (a fear of paper)?

WOULD YOU RATHER:

Suffer from Somniphobia (a fear of falling asleep) OR Coprastasophobia (a fear of becoming constipated)?

WOULD YOU RATHER:

Suffer from Geniophobia (a fear of chins) OR Genuphobia (a fear of knees and/or kneeling)?

WOULD YOU RATHER:

Suffer from Emetophobia (a fear of vomiting)
OR Aulophobia (a fear of flutes)?

WOULD YOU RATHER:

Suffer from Arachibutyrophobia (a fear of
Peanut Butter sticking to the roof of your
mouth) OR Scriptophobia (a fear of writing
in public)?

WOULD YOU RATHER:

Suffer from Pentheraphobia (a fear of your
mother-in-law) OR Doraphobia (a fear of
touching the skin or fur of an animal)?

WOULD YOU RATHER:

Suffer from Brontophobia (a fear of thunder)
OR Tapheophobia (a fear of being buried
alive)?

WOULD YOU RATHER:

Suffer from Kathisophobia (a fear of sitting down) OR Hypengyophobia (a fear of responsibility)?

WOULD YOU RATHER:

Suffer from Lutraphobia (a fear of otters) OR Pupaphobia (a fear of puppets)?

WOULD YOU RATHER:

Suffer from Alektorophobia (a fear of chickens) OR Linonophobia (a fear of string)?

Record Breakers

Break the record for most toilet seats broken over your head in one minute OR most straws placed in your mouth in one minute?

WOULD YOU RATHER:

Break the record for heaviest weight lifted by an eye socket OR the heaviest weight of bees covering your body?

WOULD YOU RATHER:

Break the record for crushing watermelons with your thighs OR most snails on your face?

WOULD YOU RATHER:

Break the record for the most cockroaches eaten in one minute OR most armpits and feet sniffed?

WOULD YOU RATHER:

Break the record for hardest kick to the groin
(you're the one being kicked) OR largest
scorpion held in the mouth?

WOULD YOU RATHER:

Break the record for most maggots moved by
mouth in one hour OR most clothes pegs
clipped to face in one minute?

WOULD YOU RATHER:

Break the record for farthest marshmallow nose-blow OR most socks put on one foot in one minute?

WOULD YOU RATHER:

Break the record for furthest distance on a unicycle in 24hrs OR heaviest car balanced on head?